T0014254

Published by
Lion Children's Books
www.lionhudson.com
Part of the SPCK Group
SPCK, 36 Causton Street, London, SW1P 4ST

ISBN 978 0 7459 9796 4 (hardback)
ISBN 978 0 7459 9798 8 (paperback)
ISBN 978 0 7459 9797 1 (paperback pack of 5)

First edition 2023

Extracts from *Common Worship: Services and Prayers* are
copyright © The Archbishops' Council, 2000, and are
reproduced by permission. All rights reserved.
copyright@churchofengland.org

A catalogue record for this book is available from
the British Library

Printed and bound in China, November 2022, LH54
Printed on paper from sustainable sources

To

. . . .

From

. . . .

Welcome
to the
Lord's Prayer

Bob Hartman
Illustrated by Raffaella Ligi

LION
CHILDREN'S

"Teach us to pray," Jesus' disciples asked him. And so, like any good teacher, in that time and in that place, Jesus taught them a prayer – a prayer that someone may well have taught you too. We call it the "Lord's Prayer" now.

Some people call it the "Model Prayer" and some people call it the "Our Father". It is a pretty good place to start, because that's where the prayer begins.

Our Father

What a beginning! God is not someone
far away or someone who is not interested
in us.

No, God is someone who made us, and
who loves us, and cares for us – just like the
very best kind of father cares for his children.
Did you spot that God is "our" Father, too,
not just "my" Father?

God didn't make us to live alone and to look out for ourselves. No, he made the world to be all about three important relationships – with him, and with one other, and with nature. It's all about "us", not "me"!

9

in heaven,

Now, you might think that heaven is far away, but that's not what the Bible says. Heaven isn't somewhere among the clouds, high up in the sky.

No, the distance between heaven and earth is like drawing back a curtain. It's right there! God is that close! But he is wonderfully different from us, for sure.

hallowed (holy) be your name,

"Hallowed" or "holy" means "special", "set apart", "sacred". If those words seem hard to understand, then consider what happens when people in the Bible get a glimpse of God. Their mouths drop open. They can hardly believe their eyes. They tremble – partly with fear, partly with joy. They are knocked out by just how amazing God is. They want to fall to their knees, praise, and worship him. That is what the angels do too! The God who is our Father, and the God who is holy, is also the God who is our king, and he deserves our praise.

your kingdom come,
your will be done,
on earth as in heaven.

Since God made the world, and God made us, it makes sense that he knows exactly what we need to do to live the best possible life. That is why the prayer is that we should serve him and follow him as our king, here on earth, exactly like the angels in heaven do.

We should trust God too, because, having
made us, he knows exactly what we need.

What we need is not to be greedy! That is why
the prayer says:

Give us today our daily bread.

God asked the children of Israel to trust him to provide for them when he gave them a kind of bread called "manna". It only lasted a day, so they couldn't save it, hoard it, and pile up more than others had. They had to trust God, day by day. The prayer is that we do that too.

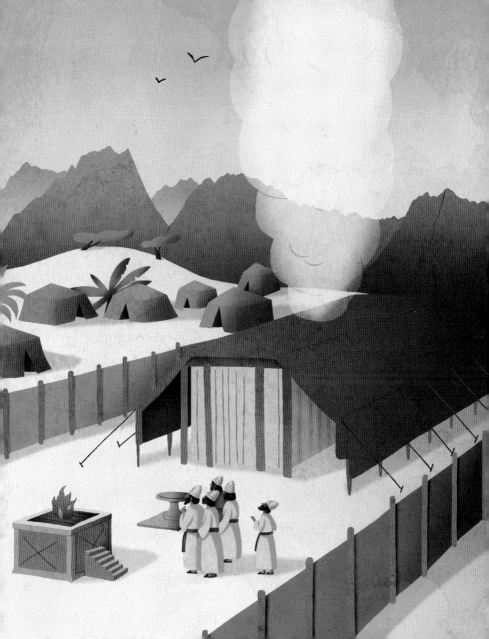

But we won't always do what God wants us to do, will we? So the prayer says:

**Forgive us our sins
as we forgive those
who sin against us.**

21

22

Remember those three relationships: with God, with one another, and with the world that God made? We do things to damage those relationships. Everybody does. We hurt others and we are hurt. But through the death of Jesus, God forgives those hurts, so that those relationships can be made good again. He asks us to follow his example and forgive one another, so that hurting and being hurt turns into forgiving and being forgiven!

Lead us not
into temptation
but deliver us
from evil.

The prayer is that we trust God to guide our lives in just the right way. It's not about each of us deciding what is best for "me". It's not about being our own little kings and queens, making up our own rules. Giving in to the temptation to do things "my" way spelled disaster for Adam and Eve and everyone who came after them.

This prayer is about trusting our Holy God and Father to help us when we are tempted to do what's wrong. Trusting him to show us the very best way to live, and to love one another, and to care for the world that he made.

For the kingdom, the power,
and the glory are yours
now and for ever.
Amen.

The prayer ends with a shout of praise –
a celebration of just how incredible God is.

It is also an assurance that all we pray for,
and all we experience with our Holy Father
and king, is not just for now but for ever.

Welcome to the Lord's Prayer!

Our Father in heaven,
hallowed (holy) be your name,
your kingdom come,
your will be done,
on earth as in heaven.
Give us today our daily bread.
Forgive us our sins
as we forgive those who sin against us.
Lead us not into temptation
but deliver us from evil.
For the kingdom, the power,
and the glory are yours
now and for ever.
Amen.